Table of Contents

Conversion Lesson #1:

Mindset of an optimizer

This is lesson no. 1 where we are just getting warmed up.

In order to achieve our goals, we need to be clear on what we're doing here. What is conversion optimization? What's the end goal?

Is it higher conversion rates? Not really. Reduce your prices to 99 cents for every product, and your conversion rates will go up immediately. But you'll probably go out of business.

So "conversion optimization" itself is a misnomer - we should NOT optimize for conversions alone. Even the people who named it dislike the name now.

So what is it about then?

It's about growth.

The question to ask is this: How do we optimize our website so that our business will grow?

As SEO is increasingly difficult (good luck trying to out compete anyone if you're just getting started) and pay-per-click costs increasingly more expensive (AdWords, Facebook, you name it) - it's getting harder and harder to grow. It's hard to make paid customer acquisition profitable since it just costs too much.

The lever you can't do without in this game is conversion optimization (and we should call it 'growth optimization' instead). It's essential for growth. If you can acquire customers more cheaply - from any channel- than your competitors, you can grow faster.

It's about better marketing

There are 2 approaches to improving a website.

1. You go in and change what you think might be a good idea to change - mainly on the home page - and hope the sales will go up.

2. You start by figuring out which pages cause the biggest drop-offs - where the flow is stuck. Once you understand WHERE the problem is, you proceed to identifying WHAT the problem is.

    You seek to understand your customers better - their needs, sources of hesitation, conversations going on inside their minds. You gather whatever quantifiable data you can to understand what people are doing on the site, and the impact each individual widget or form field has on the revenue.

Yeah - that really is a no-brainer choice. You can do way better marketing if your messaging and offers actually correspond to what the market wants, and if you focus on pages where you have the biggest leaks.

BUT - most of the world still operates using the first approach. I talk to a lot of executives in my line of work. You'd be surprised how many well-known companies are still completely in the dark. They do some things well in general - or they wouldn't be well-known - but the wasted opportunity is huge.

Some of it is due to ignorance, some of it due to resistance to change (even testing opposition). Companies run by leaders with optimization opposition will eventually be eaten by the competition.

So how does one become a good optimizer?

STEP #1: Accept these inalienable truths

1. **Your opinion doesn't matter.** If there's anything I've learned in

this business, it's that opinions don't make money. My friend and mentor Craig Sullivan likes to say that "opinions are like assholes - everybody's got one". You are not your customer, and you have lots of different kinds of customers.

Implement this rule in your company: whenever somebody voices an opinion, they have to preface it by saying: "In my insignificant, unsupported, baseless opinion". That will set the right tone for the importance of whatever is to follow.

2. **You don't know what will work**. Every now and then you meet someone - typically someone (self-)important - who will proclaim to know what works, what should be changed on the site for improved results.

   Well, they're full of shit. Nobody knows what will work. If we did, we'd all be billionaires. Unfortunately, magic crystal balls don't exist. That's why we need split testing.

3. **There are no magic templates for higher conversions.** There's no universally best product page layout, no "best home page design" layout. There are no things that always work. Marketers that tell you otherwise by selling "tests that always win" ebooks are just after your money. For every best practice you find, I will show you 10 tests where it failed.

   Best practices work - but only on half the sites. You don't know which half your site belongs to. Stop thinking in tactics, and start thinking in processes. As the saying goes, if you can't describe what you're doing as a process, you don't know what you're doing.

Once you accept these truths, it's far easier to move ahead. We humans like our egos - and we like to tickle our egos. But we need to move past that. Conversion optimization is very humbling in this regard. I have seen too many times my ideas - that I was super confident in - fail badly in A/B tests.

I've been in this business for many years - but when I have to predict a winner in a test, I get it right about 60-70% of the time. Only slightly better than flipping a coin. Not nearly good enough.

So stop guessing, and stop liking your own ideas so much. Separate yourself from opinions.

STEP #2: Turn your unsupported and baseless opinions into data-informed, educated hypotheses

You need to move away from random guessing, and focus instead on KNOWING what's happening, and understanding WHY.

Conversion optimization will be very effective once you move away from testing crap that doesn't matter, and start approaching it like the process that it is:

Set goals → Set up measurement and gather data → Analyze data → Turn data into insights → Turn insights into prioritized hypotheses → Test your hypotheses → Get data from tests → Back to data analysis. And round and round we go.

Supplemental reading:

http://conversionxl.com/your-design-sucks-copy-continuous-optimization/

http://conversionxl.com/sell-conversion-rate-optimization-to-your-boss/

http://conversionxl.com/stop-copying-your-competitors-they-dont-know-what-theyre-doing-either/

Conversion Lesson #2: Conversion Research

As we learned from lesson #1 - opinions are out, data-informed approach is in.

Or if you're not convinced yet, answer me this: would you rather have a doctor operate on you based on an opinion, or careful examination and tests? Exactly. We are conversion doctors, and websites are our patients - if you like that metaphor.

So how do we go about gathering and analyzing data?

The thing is that we don't just need more data, we need better data. Data that we can act on. For every piece of data that you gather, you need to know exactly how you're going to use it. Forget "nice to have" data. "Must have" only.

So we need to be smart about it. Data is only useful if it can lead to insights. Insight is something we can turn into a test hypothesis. If we have too much data, it causes analysis paralysis - too overwhelmed by the sheer volume of data - so we won't do anything.

Over the years of doing this, I developed a conversion research framework that I use - and it works really, really well. I call it ResearchXL.

_Research_XL™ framework

You can use this framework for each and every optimization project. It's industry-agnostic - doesn't matter if the site you're working on is a B2B lead gen, SaaS, ecommerce or non-profit site. The process you use to get higher conversions is exactly the same across all websites.

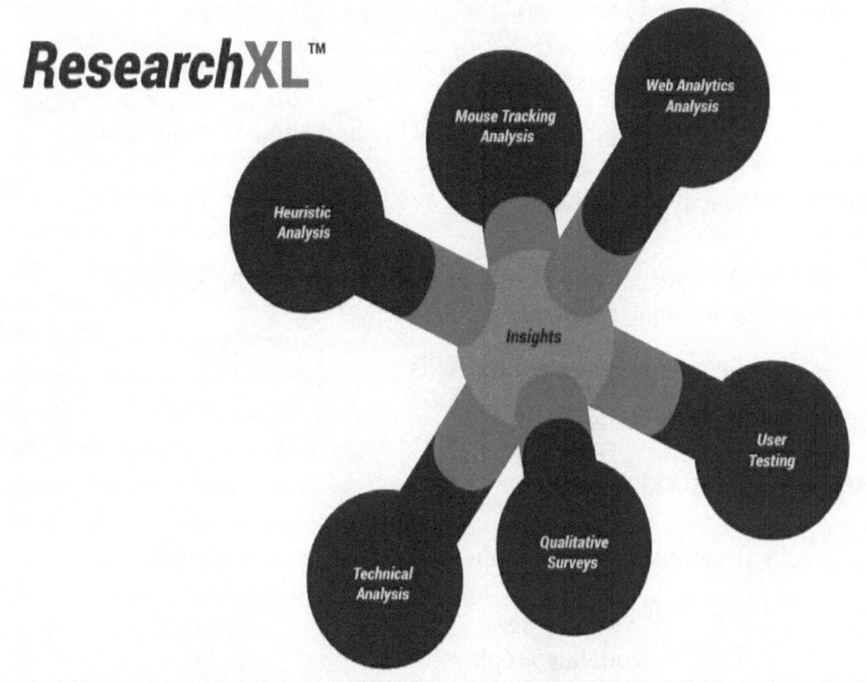

There are 6 steps of data gathering and analysis, followed by creating a master sheet of all found issues that we then turn into action items.

It might sound scarier than it is. Over the next days and weeks we'll look at each step individually. This lesson focuses on the big picture + first 2 steps.

Use the framework as your tool, your guide, your process map.
It looks like this:

Step 1. Technical analysis

- Cross-browser testing
- Cross-device testing
- Conversion rate per device / browser
- Speed analysis

Step 2. Heuristic analysis

- Identify "areas of interest"
- Check key pages for relevancy, motivation, friction issues

Step 3. Web analytics analysis

- Analytics health check: is everything being measured, is everything accurate
- Set up measurement for KPIs
- Identify leaks

Step 4. Mouse tracking analysis

- Heat maps & click maps
- Scroll maps
- User session video replays

Step 5. Qualitative research / surveys

- Customer surveys
- Web traffic surveys
- Chat logs
- Interviews

Step 6. User testing

- Identify usability & clarity issues, sources of friction

Step 7. Sum-up

- Categorize and prioritize each issue, translate into a test hypothesis

Explaining the framework

Let's now dive in to each specific element of the framework. In this lesson we'll cover the first two steps.

Step 1: Technical analysis

Don't even think about anything else until we've fixed all the technical stuff. Bugs are your main conversion killer.

You think your site works perfectly - both in terms of user experience and functionality - with every browser and device? Probably not.

This is a low-hanging fruit, one that you can make a lot of money on (think 12 month perspective). Open up your site in non-mainstream browser (e.g. IE9) and some non-mainstream device (e.g. Nexus tablet) and conduct a walkthrough of your site. Find any annoyances? Fix them.

You don't need to own all the devices and you don't need all browsers installed on your machine. Use services like https://crossbrowsertesting.com/and http://www.browserstack.com/.

Open up your Google Analytics and go to Audience -> Technology -> Browser & OS report.

You will see conversion rate (for the goal of your choice) per browser. Note: You must look at the one device category at a time - so apply a device segments first: desktop only, tablet only and mobile only. You can't pile all device categories into one, or you will be fooled by averages.

You need to drill down to a specific browser version (e.g. IE8, IE9 etc) - and see if a particular browser converts less than others. So if IE10 and IE9 convert at 5%, but IE8 converts at 2%, you have a reason to believe that there are some cross-browser issues there. Now fire up IE8 and go figure out what's up.

"But no one uses IE8 (or whatever lesser used browser)!"

That's an opinion. If you find a low-performing browser that's not used very much, do this:

- Look up the number of IE8 visitors per month.

- Look up the average transaction amount. Let's assume it's $50 for this example.

- Calculate: if IE8 (currently converting at 2%) would convert the same as IE10 (currently 5%), how many more transactions would we have over 6 month period? Let's pretend that we'd get 200 transactions more over 6 months.

- Multiply that number with avg transaction amount ($50), so 200x50=$10,000

- How much time will it take to identify and fix the bug? 3 hours? Is 3 hours of developer time more or less than $10k? If less, fix the damn bugs!

Repeat this flow with each browser that's converting sub-optimally.

Making money already!

If you're thinking: "this does not sound like conversion optimization!", you're wrong. Remember: our job is to optimize our website so our business would grow. Plugging cross-browser & cross-device leaks equals growth.

Next up: **speed analysis.**

The goal: figure out overall website speed, and analyze load speed per page.

Key thing to know - there's a difference between "page load time" and "page interactive time". The first one means "seconds until every element on the page has done loading" and second one means "seconds until the site is usable". The latter is much more important, it's the key metric you want to pay attention to.

If the site loads within 3 seconds, you're doing fine. Up to 7 seconds? Quite typical, can be improved. More than 10 seconds? Gotta do something!

Where to look for site speed data:

Google Analytics: Behavior → Site Speed → Page Timings. You want to look at page load time and page interactive time per page - starting with the ones that have the most traffic (== affect the largest number of users).

Mark down all URLs that load with sub-optimal speed.

Use Google PageSpeed Insights (can also be accessed from within GA). Enter every URL you wrote down, and it will list all the found issues. Forward those to your front-end developer - and ask to fix every single one of them.

Use Pingdom or similar to see the number of requests, and how long each one takes. This helps you identify slow-loading scripts, especially those loaded from external domains. Keeping the number of scripts the page loads (called "requests") down is essential for better load times.

Always use caching, compression and minifiction (if the website runs on Apache web server, have your server guys install PageSpeed module).

Read this article I wrote on the key speed optimizations you want to do on most sites: http://conversionxl.com/11-low-hanging-fruits-for-increasing-website-speed-and-conversions/

Step 2: Heuristic analysis

This is as close as we get to using opinions to optimize. But - it's way more productive than just randomly sharing stupid ideas.

Let's start with a definition: heuristic analysis is an experience-based assessment where the outcome is not guaranteed to be optimal, but might be good enough. It's main advantage - speed. It can be done fairly quickly.

In essence this is us - optimizers - reviewing a website, page by page, based on our experience of what we've seen work before, "best practices" and stuff like that. BUT - we do it in a very organized, structured manner.

AND - most importantly - whatever we identify or discover through heuristic analysis is not the truth (since it's still kind of an educated opinion). The outcome of it is what I call "areas of interest". And in our next phases of conversion research - qualitative and quantitative research - we seek to validate or invalidate the findings.

What does the structured website review look like? We assess each page for a certain set of criteria:

- **Relevancy:** does the page meet user expectation - both in terms of content and design? How can it match what they want even more?

- **Clarity:** Is the content / offer on this page as clear as possible? How can we make it clearer, simpler?

- **Value:** is it communicating value to the user? Can we do better? Can we increase user motivation?

- **Friction:** what on this page is causing doubts, hesitations and uncertainties? What makes the process difficult? How can we simplify? We can't reduce friction entirely, we can only minimize it.

- **Distraction:** what's on the page that is not helping the user take action? Is anything unnecessarily drawing attention? If it's not motivation, it's friction - and thus it might be a good idea to get rid of it.

Read more: http://conversionxl.com/how-to-increase-sales-online-the-checklist/

So during the process of heuristic analysis you have to avoid random comments, and strictly stick to assessing the page for named criteria - writing down your "findings".

Heuristic analysis works best when done in a group - include fellow optimizers, designers, usability people, copywriters, and janitors. Just remember to explain the rules to everyone at the start.

I personally find it most effective to annotate findings on screenshots - so it's clear what we mean. There is no right way of doing it. You can use Jing to capture screenshots and add comments on top of it, you can use PowerPoint or a collaborative annotation tool like Framebench (you can write comments on the same screenshots at the same time while using your respective computers). The tool does not matter.

Example, executed in Google Docs:

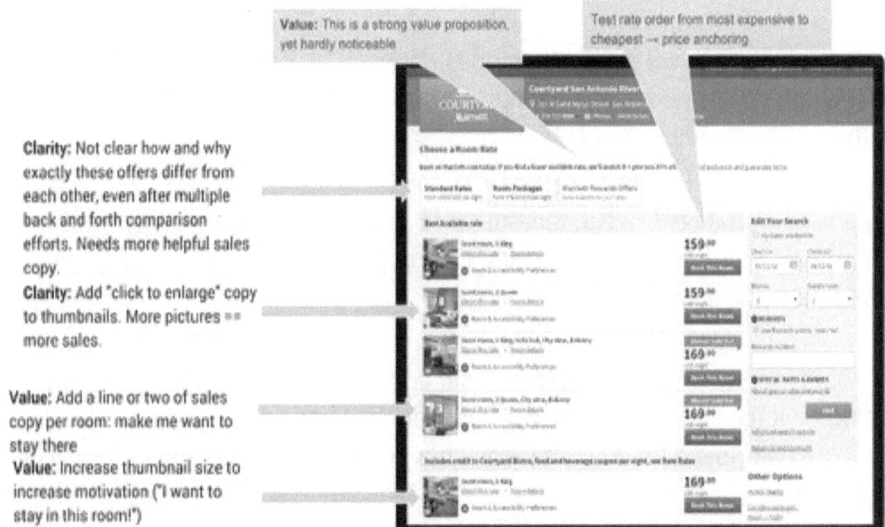

And remember - whatever you write down is merely "areas of interest".

When you start digging in the analytics data and putting together user testing plans and what not, make sure you investigate that stuff - with the intention to validate or invalidate whatever you found.

Conversion Lesson #3:
Google Analytics for CRO

Google Analytics is a HUGE topic. Before even thinking about specific tactics and what not, it's important to understand the big picture of how to use analytics in conversion optimization. This is what this lesson is about.

When doing optimization work, Google Analytics is your best friend. If you're not very skilled at it - most marketers aren't - you're missing out. You need to take the time to learn. Your career depends on it.

Gone are the days when a brilliant idea - a result of a brainstorm in the marketing department - was enough. Now you need to know the specific impact of every idea.

You have a strategy? Great, measure it. You added a new feature to your website. Well - how many are using it? Are people using it more likely or less likely to convert?

If your Google Analytics skills max out at checking how much traffic you're getting, which country they're coming from and how many minutes on average they spend on your site, you know nothing. This is useless for CRO purposes.

Note for analytics newbies: Google itself has released a pretty good introductory course called <u>Digital Analytics Fundamentals</u> - I suggest you take it.

What can we learn from Google Analytics?

This topic would take a three day workshop, but for this essentials course I will point out the key stuff.

Always approach analytics with a problem: you need to know in advance what you want to know, and what are you going to change / do based on the answer. If nothing, then you don't need it.

In a nutshell, we can learn:

- what people are doing,
- the impact and performance of every feature, widget, page,
- where the site is leaking money,

… but we won't know why. Heuristic analysis and qualitative research are your best attempts at figuring out the 'why'. Analytics is more like 'what', 'where' and 'how much'.

Follow the data!, they say. Well, truth be told, data won't tell you anything. It is up to you to pull the insights out of the data. And this requires practice. As with everything - the more time you spend at looking at data, and trying to make sense of it, the better you'll get at it.

It's time well spent, no matter what. If I were a (full-stack) marketer today, and not analytics-savvy, I'd fear for my future. You need to love analytics. Remember, love at first sight rarely happens. Spend more time together.

Averages lie - look at segments, distributions, comparisons

Most companies market to their average user, most marketers look at average numbers in analytics. But that's wrong.

So if your buyer #1 is a 12 year girl from Finland, and buyer #2 is a 77 year old dude from Spain, the average is sexually confused 30-something in Austria. That's the market you think you're after. See what I mean?

Your "average" conversion rate is 4.2%. But it becomes much more interesting if you look at it per device category segment - desktop, tablet, mobile. You now have a much better picture.

Instead of looking at a static number, look at distributions.

Distributions will also insightful in the case of "totals". So instead of just looking at total transactions:

Transactions

2,617

You could look at the number when it's distributed by "visits to transaction", and learn that most people are ready to buy during their first visit:

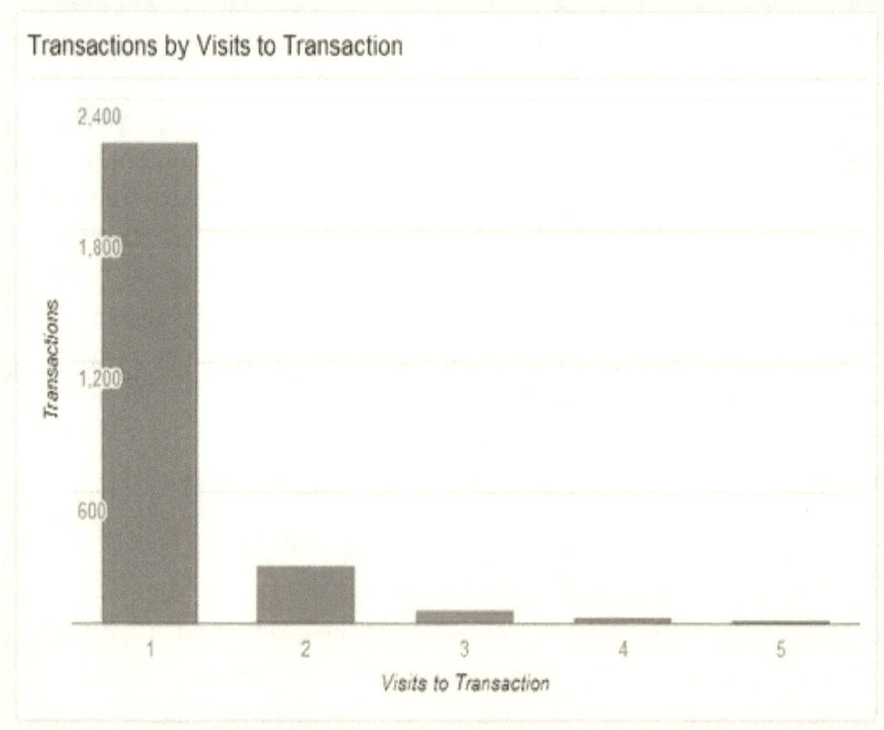

And always, always use absolute numbers next to ratios. For instance if landing page A results in 8% conversion rate and landing page B has 2% conversion rate, you need to know the absolute number of conversions to know if you can trust the ratio.

If the total number of actions is less than 100, be very suspicious of it - the ratio is probably wrong (sample size not big enough).

Measuring the important stuff

I see a lot of Google Analytics setups. Hundreds and hundreds. Most companies struggle with the proper setup. Most companies are not measuring everything that matters.

You need to measure all the important stuff. Every action people can take on your site. Especially your KPIs.

A key performance indicator (KPI) is a metric that helps you understand how you are doing against your objectives. A metric is a number.

So your KPIs might be 'conversion rate for email captures', 'revenue per visitor', 'number of downloads per month'.

There are useful metrics, and useless metrics. The job of a metric is to provide actionable insight. You need to be able to look at a metric, ask "so what"? – and have an answer.

Let's say you run an ecommerce site. Your 'time on site' is 3:42, 15 seconds less than it was last month. So what? Umm… well nothing I guess. So stop paying attention to it! Focus on metrics that do matter.

In most cases 'time on site' is quite a useless metric for an ecommerce site. Whether people spend more time or less time on a site does not correlate with the amount of money you're making. You should NOT optimize for 'people spending more time on the site'. Focus on 'revenue per visitor' instead.

So - make a list of all possible desired actions a user can take, such as:

- click on 'add to cart',
- change sort order from 'featured' to 'best-selling',
- interact with widget X,

- narrow down product selection via price filters,
- use site search,
- use comparison tool,
- join email list,
- buy stuff,
- and so on.
- Now make a list of the bad stuff that can happen:
- enter incorrect login,
- see error messages when filling out billing info,
- error 404 - page not found,
- remove product from cart,

etc.

Next - set up measurement for all of these items. Some of the stuff you might be able to measure by setting thank you page URL as a Goal, for most of this stuff you will need event tracking.

Here's an example. An ecommerce site has a feature. I set up a segment for people that use this feature. Now I'm comparing site average ecommerce performance to this specific segment:

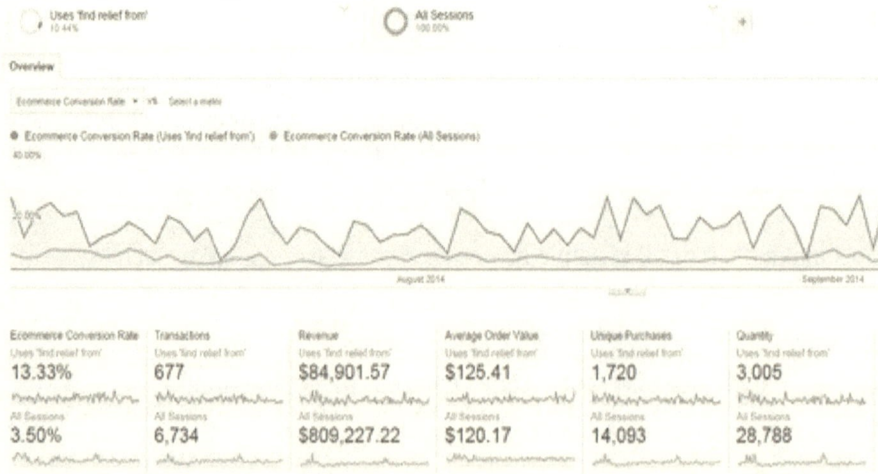

What do we see? People who use this specific feature convert almost 4x better, and spend slightly more money. That's an insight!

There could be lots of reasons for this - we don't know for sure just by looking at these numbers. But right now ~10% of users use this feature. What would happen if we got 20% to use it? This insight can be turned into a test hypothesis.

If we didn't measure this stuff, we would have no idea. No data-driven hypothesis.

If you sell stuff for money on your site, you have a shopping cart system, products at different price points, then you absolutely need to have ecommerce tracking configured on your site. You need a developer for this. If you don't have it, you're completely blind when you don't have to be.

If you have NO GOALS set up - you're a voluntary idiot. Your analytics are 100% useless. Might as well give up now. Or - get your act together, and start measuring stuff.

You need to have goals set up for all key actions (purchase, lead generation etc). Don't set goals for stupid shit like "visits about page" - analytics measures visits to pages anyway.

And - you absolutely need to have funnels set up (unless everything happens on a single page): Product page -> Cart Page -> Checkout step 1 -> Step 2 -> Step 3 -> Thank you.

I suggest you read this article very carefully as it has step-by-step instructions for setting up your Google Analytics config.

For setting up event tracking you need one of these three options:

1. Use Google Tag Manager to set up event tracking (the best option), naturally requires that you have GTM already set up. Read this article to learn more about tag managers, and read this post on using Google Tag Manager. If you don't run your analytics through a tag manager, you're being silly and unnecessarily complicating things.
2. Learn to code, so you can manually add event tracking scripts to

your site, wherever needed.

3. Tell your developer to set up event tracking for everything on your list.

Ideally you only pursue option #1 - it's the fastest and most sustainable option. Having to go through a developer every time - and hard code each event tracking script - is a pain in the butt, and will likely cause problems down the line.

If you work with a Google Analytics setup that was done by someone else, you need to start with an analytics health check.

In a nutshell: health check is a series of analytics and instrumentation checks that answers the following questions:

- *"Does it collect what we need?"*
- *"Can we trust this data?"*
- *"Where are the holes?"*
- *"Is there anything that can be fixed?"*
- *"Is anything broken?"*
- *"What reports should be avoided?"*

The truth is that nearly all analytics configurations are broken. Take this very seriously. See if everything that needs to be measured is measured, multiple views set up, funnel and goal data accurate (calculate funnel performance manually via Behavior -> Site Content reports, and compare to funnel data as well as your back-end sales reporting tool).

If you see bounce rates under 10%, you can be sure that this is due to broken setup - either GA code loaded twice, or some event triggered right away that's not set to non-interactive.

I know I'm not being 1-2-3 here, but this is merely an essentials course - and you wouldn't want this email to be 10,000 words long. It's important to know that this is an issue, and you can do your own investigation from here.

Finding the leaks

Okay - time to find out where you are losing your money. Where's the flow stuck?

We need to identify specific pages (e.g. Free & Clear Shampoo 12-oz bottle) as well as specific steps (e.g. Product pages) where we are losing money.

Maybe category pages are the problem - not enough people won't click through to product pages. Or perhaps they get to product pages, but only 1% adds anything to the cart. Or maybe some product pages work really well, but some suck (which ones?). Or maybe plenty add products to the cart, and make it almost all the way to the end - but drop out as soon as credit card is required.

Where are the biggest leaks? Where should we start optimizing? (In most cases it's not your home page).

This is your checklist to find out:

- Check the funnel performance
- Check conversions per browser version
- Check conversions and bounce rate per device
- Identify high traffic & high bounce / high exit rate pages
- High traffic / High bounce / Low conversion Landing Pages
- Which screen resolution boosts bounce rates?
- High traffic / Low speed Pages
- Check user flows
- Look at conversions per traffic source
- Analyze new vs returning

I've written about this checklist at length here.

Conversion Lesson #4:
Mouse tracking and heatmaps

Now - let's get started with lesson number 4. In a nutshell: we can record what people do with their mouse / trackpad, and can quantify that information. Some of it might be insightful.

There are many tools that enable you to do this stuff, and some of them call the stuff differently. Some tools - like Crazyegg for instance - calls a click map "heat map". So always check the tools documentation to see what they call what, how they define things.

Very important: like with A/B testing, you need enough sample size per page / screen before you can trust any results. A rough ballpark would be 2000-3000 pageviews per design screen. If the heat map is based off like 34 users, do not trust any of it.

Heat maps

What is a heat map? It's a graphical representation of data where the individual values contained in a matrix are represented as colors. Red equals lots of action, and blue equals no action. And then there are colors in between.

When people say 'heat map', they typically mean hover map. It shows you areas that people have hovered over with their mouse cursor - and the idea is that people look where they hover, so it's kind of like poor man's eye tracking.

The accuracy of this thing is always questionable. People might be looking at stuff that they don't hover over, and might hovering over stuff that gets very little attention - and hence the heat map is inaccurate. Maybe it's accurate, maybe it's not. How do you know? You don't.

That's why I typically ignore this types of heatmaps. I mean I do look at the info if it's there - to see if it confirms my own observations / suspicions (or not), but I don't put much weight on it.

There are also tools that algorithmically analyze your user interface, and generate heat maps off of that. They take into account stuff like colors, contrast, size of elements. While I don't fully trust these either (not based on actual users), I don't think they're any less trustworthy than your hover maps.

Using algorithmic tools is especially a good idea if you lack traffic. It gives you instant results. Check out Feng GUI (relatively cheap) and EyeQuant(best in class).

Click maps

A click map is a visual representation, aggregated data of where people click. Red equals lots of clicks.

You can see where people click also with Google Analytics - and I actually prefer that. Provided that you have enhanced link attribution turned on and set up, Google Analytics overlay is great (but some people prefer to see it on a click map type of visual).

And if you go to Behavior -> Site Content -> All pages, and click on an URL, you can open up Navigation Summary for any URL - where people came from, and where they went after. Highly useful stuff.

OK - back to click maps. So there is one useful bit here I like - you can see clicks on non-links. If there's an image or text that people think is a link or want to be a link, they'll click on it. And you can see that on a click map.

If you discover something (image, sentence etc) that people want to click on, but isn't a link, then:

- A) make it into a link,
- B) don't make it look like a link.

Attention maps

Some tools - like SessionCam for instance - provide attention maps.

It shows which areas of the page have been viewed the most by the user's browser with full consideration of the horizontal and vertical scrolling activity.

What makes this useful is that it takes account different screen sizes and resolutions, and shows which part of the page has been viewed the most within the user's browser. Understanding attention can help you assess the effectiveness of the page design, especially above the fold area.

You can see if key pieces of information - both in terms of text and visuals - are in the area that's visible to almost all users.

I consider this far more useful than any mouse movement or click heatmap.

Scroll map

This shows you scroll depth - how far down people scroll. Can be very useful.

It's absolutely normal that the longer the page, the less people make it all the way down. So once you acknowledge this, it makes it easier to prioritize content. What's must-have and what's nice-to-have. Must have content must be higher.

Also if your page is longer, you probably want to sprinkle multiple calls to action in there - look at your scroll map to see where are the biggest drop-off points.

Analyzing the scroll map will also help you decide where you need to tweak your design. If you have strong lines or color changes (e,g. white background becomes orange), those are called 'logical ends' - often people think that whatever follows is no longer connected to what came before.

So you can add better eye paths and visual cues to spots where scrolling activity seems to drop heavily.

User session replays

You can record video sessions of people going through your site. It's kind of like user testing, but has no script and no audio. But people are risking with their actual money - so it can be more insightful.

You don't need a million visitors to record user sessions – this is almost like qualitative data. Use tools like Inspectlet (great), SessionCam (terrible UI, but a workhorse), or Clicktale to record user sessions, and watch your actual visitors interact with your site. Some basic heatmap tools like Crazyegg don't even have this feature.

Session replays are extremely useful for observing how people fill out forms on your site. You can configure event tracking for Google Analytics, but it won't provide the level of insight that user session replay videos do.

One of our customers has an online resume building service. The process consists of 4 steps, and there was a huge drop-off in the first step. We watched videos to understand how people were filling out the form. We noticed the first step had too many form fields, and we saw that out of all the people who started filling out the form, the majority of users stopped at this question:

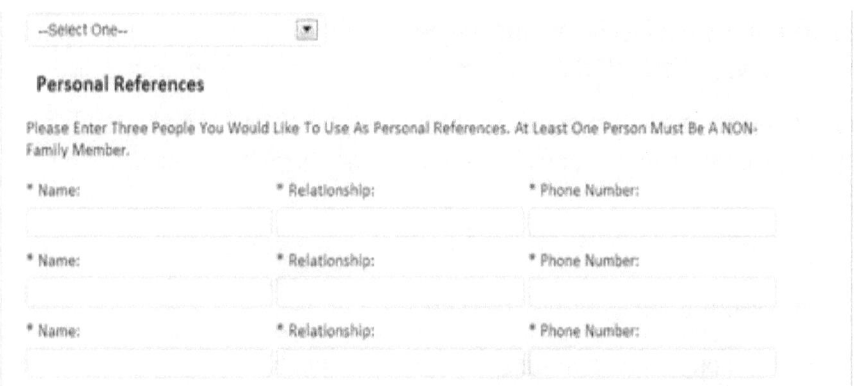

Personal references! The form asked for 3. Most people had none. So they abandoned the process. Solution: get rid of the references part!

Very difficult to learn this without watching the videos.

I typically spend half a day watching videos for a new client site. Not any random videos, but where they visited key pages. Try to see what's different between converters and non-converters etc.

Form analytics

Not exactly mouse tracking, but several mouse tracking tools like Inspectletor Clicktale have this feature. Or use a standalone tool like Formisimo.

These tools will analyze form performance down to individual form fields.

- Which form fields cause the most error messages?
- Which form field people hesitate to fill? Hesitation measured in milliseconds
- Which form fields people leave empty, even though they're required?

And so on.

If your goal is to make your forms better - and form optimization is a key part of CRO - it really adds a whole new layer of insight where you have data about each and every form field.

You can remove problematic fields, or re-word instructions, or add help text, or turn inline field labels into top aligned labels. Whatever. The main point is that you know WHERE the problem is, so you can try to address it.

No data on form fields = guessing. And your guesswork is no better that flipping a coin. And you don't want to base the success of your work on a coin toss.

Good luck!

6 more lessons to go. Getting tired yet?

You see, in conversion optimization there's so much to know. And in this free course I'm only helping you scratch the surface. But we're getting there, one step at a time.

Conversion Lesson #5:
Using Website Surveys

Let us continue with the qualitative stuff. Last lesson was about learning from your customers.

But most people on your site will not buy anything. How can we get more people to buy? One thing that helps us figure that out is website surveys.

There are 2 ways to survey your web traffic:

1. Exit surveys: hit them with a popup when they're about to leave your site.

2. On-page surveys: ask them to fill out a survey as they're on a specific page

Both are useful.

There are many tools to use that, I usually use Qualaroo, but there's alsoWebEngage and many other tools. The tool itself doesn't matter as long as it gets the job done:

- Configure which page(s) will have the survey on
- Set your own questions (no pre-written template bullshit)
- Determine the criteria for when to show the survey

If these 3 criteria are met, you're solid.

Aren't surveys annoying to people? Sure they might be to some - but the data you get out of it is well worth it. And you typically only run the surveys for a limited period of time.

What should you ask?

Remember the key: actionable data. We need information to act on.

Since our goal is to get more people to take action, start with learning about friction. What are the FUDs (fears, doubts, hesitations) they are experiencing

- while on a specific page?

Every page on your site has one job - and your survey question should be about that one page, one job.

For ecommerce product page it's to get people to click on 'add to cart'. For checkout page its to get people to take out their wallet, and enter their credit card info. And so on.

Step 1: Determine the most wanted action for the page.

Step 2: Come up with a question that asks about friction.

So for instance if this is an ecommerce product page, the goal would be cart adds. So the question to ask could be something like "What's holding you back from adding this product to the cart right now?" or "What's keeping you from buying this right now?".

You don't always know which question is the best one to ask - there is no single best question. Some questions will get far better response rates, but you won't know in advance which ones.

So try to come up with multiple different wordings to the question.

Another way to ask about friction could be "Do you have any questions that you can't find answers to?" - give them a Y/N option, and if they choose No, have them type in their question.

This is my pro tip actually: Ask all questions in the form of Y/N. It's easy to just choose Yes or No. If you hit them with a complicated question right away, less people will take the time to write. But if you start with Y/N, and only once they choose 'No', then pop the question, they're much more likely to respond.

I see 2% - 4% response rates all the time.

So instead of "what's holding you back from..." you would ask "Is there anything holding you back from ..."? Y/N. And ask to clarify.

And remember - a different question for each page (e.g. pricing page, category page etc) - that's the only way to learn about the specific friction they're experiencing on that very page.

When to pop the question?

Not right away. You want to qualify the visitor first - a bunch of your traffic has no intention to buy at all. There's nothing you can do to get them to buy. Lots of people want to drive a Tesla, few can afford the $100k.

So you only want to survey people who have demonstrated a level of engagement. Maybe there's a micro-conversion they need to complete first (e.g. join the newsletter). Or look up your average time on site, average pages per visit - and trigger the question only once they've spent above average amount of time, clicked through above average amount of pages.

You need to do some experimentation with this, there's no universal rule.

How many responses do you need?

One answer is better than none, but you don't want to put too much weight on a single response. They might be an outlier, an edge case.
So I typically try to get in at least 100 responses before even reading any. 200 is better.

How long it will take to get 100 responses depends on your traffic, so if you have a low-traffic site, you might have to do with less responses.

What to look for

As always, see if you spot any trends in the responses. See if your customer survey responses about friction are similar to web traffic survey results. You're mining for insights! See if you can validate or invalidate some of your observations from the heuristic analysis.

A bunch of people will tell you that pricing is an issue ("too expensive!") - that's to be expected. If that's a dominant response, you're either driving too much unqualified traffic to the site, or you're not doing a good enough job communicating the value of your product(s).

Conversion Lesson #6:
User Testing

Last qualitative bit in this series: user testing

The premise is simple: observe actual people use and interact with your website while they're commenting their thought process out loud. Pay attention to what they say and experience.

User testing gives you direct input on how real users use your site. You may have designed what you believe is the best user experience in the world, but watching real people interact with your site is often a humbling experience. Because you are not your user.

You can do this in-person or remote. When you do this in person - you go to test users or have them come to you - make sure you film the whole thing. Doing it remote by using online user testing tools if definitely the cheapest and fastest way to do it.

Creating user testing protocols

User testing starts with creating a test protocol - tasks that you want your test users to complete.

Online user testing tools limit one session to 15-20 minutes, so don't try to cram too many tasks into one test. Depending on your site, 4-5 tasks per test is typically enough.

What kind of tasks should they complete?

The main thing you want to assess is completing key actions, such as signing up for something and buying something. You want to create scenarios that actual users would follow, and aim to identify all the friction they experience in the process.

Maybe they're not able to find something, or can't figure out how to do XYZ, or make mistakes when filling out forms.

Remember - every "mistake" a user makes is not because they're stupid, but because your website sucks. When watching user testing videos it's easy to say "I can't believe these idiots don't see that button". But the real idiot is you for putting that button somewhere where people don't look. But that's okay - you can fix it!

In most cases you want to include 3 types of tasks in your test protocol.

- A specific task
- A broad task
- Funnel completion

So let's say you run an ecommerce site that sells clothes. Your tasks might as follow:

- Find dark jeans in size 34 under $50 (specific task)
- Find a shirt that you like (broad task)
- Buy the shirt (funnel completion)

You have users that know what they want, and users who're browsing around. This test protocol accounts for both. And funnel completion is the most important thing - you want to make purchasing as easy and obvious as possible.

Make sure you have them use dummy credit cards to complete the purchase. If you don't let them complete the full checkout process, you're missing out on critical insight.

If your platform does not allow dummy credit cards, you might want to run user tests on a staging server (if available), or get some pre-paid credit cards and share that info with testers. Once they've completed the test, just refund the money and cancel order.

Tasks to avoid

A typical rookie mistake is to form tasks as questions - "Do you feel this page is secure?" or "Would you buy from this site?". That's complete rubbish, utterly useless.

The point is to OBSERVE the user. If they comment on security voluntarily, great. If they don't, it's likely not an issue. Don't ask for their opinion on anything, just have them complete tasks and pay attention to the comments they volunteer and to how they (try to) use the website interface.

Asking whether they would buy or not is completely useless as humans are not capable of accurately predicting their future actions. It's one thing to say that you hypothetically would buy something, and it's a completely different thing to actually take out your wallet and part with your money.

Test users know that they're not risking with their actual money - so their behavior is not 100% reflective of actual buyer behavior.
Once I ran user testing for an expensive hotel chain. Test users had no problem booking rooms that cost over $500 per night. I seriously doubt they'd pay that much so easily in "real life".

Another common mistake is telling them exactly what to do. For instance "use filters to narrow down the selection". Don't do that. You just give them the goal (e.g. find stores near you), and watch what happens.

Recruiting testers

Your testers should be people from your target audience (although ANY random tester is better than no tester) that understand your offer, and might represent the people you're actually trying to sell to.

Also - it should be the very first time they're using your site. So you can't use past customers as testers. They're already familiar with your site, and have learned to use it even if it has a ton of usability issues.

If your service/product is for a wide audience (e.g. you sell shoes or fitness products), you have it easy. You can turn to services like usertesting.com or TryMyUI.com, and recruit testers from their pool. I use usertesting.com all the time with every client.

If you have a very niche audience (e.g software quality assurance testers or cancer patients on vegan diet), it can get more complicated. You can reach out to dedicated communities (e.g. forums for software testers or people with cancer), use your personal connections (friends of friends) or dedicated recruiting services (expensive).

If you do custom recruiting, you absolutely need to pay your testers, typically $25 to $50 per tester (depending on how niche they are). Or much more if they're way more niche.

How many to recruit

In most cases 5 to 10 test users is enough. 15 max - law of diminishing returns kicks in after that.

How often

You should conduct user testing every time before you roll out a major change (run tests on the staging server), or at least once a year.

Definitely at the start of every optimization project.

Once you have all the videos done, time to review them all at once. Go through the videos, take notes of every single issue.

Fix the obvious problems and test everything else. If needed, recruit another 5 test users to see if the issues were solved or any new ones were created in the process.

Conversion Lesson #7:
From data to test hypotheses

Every conversion project starts with conversion research. During the research process you complete everything we've been discussing in the previous lessons:

- Technical testing
- Heuristic analysis
- Web analytics analysis
- Mouse tracking analysis
- Customer surveys
- Web traffic surveys
- User testing

Once you go through all these, you will find identify issues - some of them severe, some minor.

Next: Allocate every finding into one of these 5 buckets:

Test

If there is an obvious opportunity to shift behavior, expose insight or increase conversion – this bucket is where you place stuff for testing. If you have traffic and leakage, this is the bucket for that issue.

Instrument

If an issue is placed in this bucket, it means we need to beef up the analytics reporting. This can involve fixing, adding or improving tag or event handling on the analytics configuration. We instrument both structurally and for insight in the pain points we've found.

Hypothesize

This is where we've found a page, widget or process that's just not working well but we don't see a clear single solution. Since we need to really shift the behaviour at this crux point, we'll brainstorm hypotheses. Driven by evidence and data, we'll create test plans to find the answers to the questions and change the conversion or KPI figure in the desired direction.

Just Do It - JFDI

This is a bucket for issues where a fix is easy to identify or the change is a no-brainer. Items marked with this flag can either be deployed in a batch or as part of a controlled test. Stuff in here requires low effort or are micro-opportunities to increase conversion and should be fixed.

Investigate

You need to do some testing with particular devices or need more information to triangulate a problem you spotted. If an item is in this bucket, you need to ask questions or do further digging.

Next: issue scoring, ranking them.

We can't do everything at once and hence need to prioritize. Why?

- Keeps you / client away from shiny things
- Focus is almost always on biggest money / lowest cost delivery
- Helps you achieve bigger wins earlier in projects
- Gives you / the client potential ROI figures
- Keeps the whole team grounded

Once we start optimizing, we start with high-priority items and leave low priority last – but eventually all of it should get done.There are many different ways you can go about it. A simple yet very useful way is to use a scoring system from 1 to 5 (1= minor issue, 5 = critically important).

In your report you should mark every issue with a star rating to indicate the level of opportunity (the potential lift in site conversion, revenue or use of features):

This rating is for a critical usability, conversion or persuasion issue that will be encountered by many visitors to the site or has high impact. Implementing fixes or testing is likely to drive significant change in conversion and revenue.

This rating is for a critical issue that may not be viewed by all visitors or has a lesser impact.

This rating is for a major usability or conversion issue that will be encountered by many visitors to the site or has a high impact.

★★

This rating is for a major usability or conversion issue that may not be viewed by all visitors or has a lesser impact.

This rating is for a minor usability or conversion issue and although is low for potential revenue or conversion value, it is still worth fixing at lower priority.

There are 2 criterias that are more important than others when giving a score:

- Ease of implementation (time/complexity/risk). Sometimes the data tells you to build a feature, but it takes months to do it. So it's not something you'd start with.

- Opportunity score (subjective opinion on how big of a lift you might get). Let's say you see that the completion rate on the checkout page is 65%. That's a clear indicator that there's lots of room for growth, and because this is a money page (payments taken here), any relative growth in percentages will be a lot of absolute dollars.

Essentially: follow the money. You want to start with things that will make a positive impact on your bottom line right away.

Be more analytical when assinging a score to items in Test and Hypothesize buckets.

Now create a table / spreadsheet with 7 columns:

Issue	Bucket	Location	Background	Action	Rating	Responsibl
Google Analytics bounce info is wrong	Instrument	Every page	Google Analytics script is loaded twice! Line 207 and 506 of the home	Remove double entry	★★★★	Jack
Missing value proposition	Hypothesize	Home page	Give reasons to buy from you	Add a prominent value proposition	★★★	Jill

Most conversion projects will have 15-30 pages full of issues. "What to test" is not a problem anymore, you will have more than enough.

Translating issues into hypotheses

Let's get on the same page by what a hypothesis is. This is a definition I like:

Hypothesis is a proposed statement made on the basis of limited evidence that can be proved or disproved and is used as a starting point for further investigation.

Every good test is based on a hypothesis. Whether a test wins or loses, we're validating a hypothesis – hence testing is essentially validated learning. And learning leads insight which leads to better hypotheses, and in turns into better results.

The better our hypothesis, the higher the chances that our treatment will work, and result in an uplift.

With a hypothesis we're matching identified problems with identified solutions while indicating the desired outcome.

Identified problem: "It's not clear what the product is, what's being sold on this page. People don't buy what they don't understand."

Proposed solution: "Let's re-write product copy so it would be easy to understand what the product is, for whom, and what the benefits are. Let's use better product photography to further improve clarity."

Hypothesis: "By improving the clarity of the product copy and overall presentation, people can better understand our offering, and we will increase the number of purchases."

All hypotheses should derived from your findings from conversion research. Don't test without hypotheses. This is basic advice, but its importance can't be overstated. There is no learning without proper hypotheses.

Next lesson: running tests!

Conversion Lesson #8:
Getting A/B testing right

In the previous lesson we talked about coming up with test hypotheses based on conversion research.

Now we need to test the issues to validate and learn. Pick a testing tool, and create treatments / alternative variations to test against the current page (control).

There's no shortage of testing tools, one even built into Google Analytics and completely free. I use Optimizely mostly, but there's also VWO, Qubit, Convert.com and many others.

A thing to keep in mind is that you want to take testing seriously, you either need the help of a developer, or you need to learn some html, css and javascript/jquery.

Testing is no joke – you have to test right. Bad testing is even worse than no testing at all – the reason is that you might be confident that solutions A, B and C work well while in reality they hurt your business.

Poor A/B testing methodologies are costing online retailers up to $13bn a year in lost revenue, according to research from Qubit. Don't take this lightly!

Very typical story of a business that does a/b testing is that they run 100 tests over the year, yet a year later their conversion rate is where it was when they began. Why? Because they did it wrong. Massive waste of time, money and human potential.

You need to make sure your sample size is big enough

In order to be confident that the results of your test are actually valid, you need to know how big of a sample size you need.

There are several calculators out there for this - like this or this.

You need a minimum number of observations for the right statistical power. Using the number you get from the sample size calculators as a ballpark is perfectly valid, but the test may not be as powerful as you had originally planned. The only real danger is in stopping the test early after looking at preliminary results. There's no penalty to have a larger sample size (only takes more time).

As a very rough ballpark I typically recommend ignoring your test results until you have at least 350 conversions per variation (or more - depending on the needed sample size).

If you want to analyze your test results across segments, you need even more conversions. It's a good idea to run tests targeting a specific segment, e.g. you have separate tests for desktop, tablets and mobile.

Once your test has enough sample size, we want to see if one or more variations is better than Control. For this we look at statistical significance.

Statistical significance (also called statistical confidence) is the probability that a test result is accurate and not due to just chance alone. Noah from 37Signals said it well:

"Running an A/B test without thinking about statistical confidence is worse than not running a test at all—it gives you false confidence that you know what works for your site, when the truth is that you don't know any better than if you hadn't run the test."

Most researchers use the 95% confidence level before making any conclusions. At 95% confidence level the likelihood of the result being random is very small (5%). Basically we're saying "this change is not a fluke or caused by chance, it probably happened due to the changes we made".

When an A/B testing dashboard (in Optimizely or a similar tool) says there is a "95% chance of beating original", it's asking the following question: Assuming there is no underlying difference between A and B, how often will we see a difference like we do in the data just by chance? The answer to that question is called the significance level, and "statistically significant results" mean that the significance level is low, e.g. 5% or 1%. Dashboards usually take the complement of this (e.g. 95% or 99%) and report it as a "chance of beating the original" or something like that.

If the results are not statistically significant, the results might be caused by random factors and there's no relationship between the changes you made and the test results (this called the null hypothesis).

But don't confuse statistical significance with validity

Once your testing tool says you've achieved 95% statistical significance (or higher), that doesn't mean anything if you don't have enough sample size. Achieving significance is not a stopping rule for a test.

Read this blog post to learn why. It's very, very important.

Duration of the test

For some high-traffic sites you would get the needed sample size in a day or two. But that is not a representative sample – it does not include a full business cycle, all week days, weekends, phase of the moon, various traffic sources, your blog publishing and email newsletter schedule and all other variables.

So for a valid test both conditions – adequate sample size + long enough time to include all factors (full business cycle, better yet 2 cycles) – should be met. For most businesses this is 2 to 4 weeks.

No substitution for experience

Start running tests now.

There's quite a bit to know about all this, but the content above will already make you smarter about running tests than most marketers.

Conversion Lesson #9:
Learning from test results

You've identified a page that is leaking money. Thanks to qualitative research, heuristic analysis and other insights you've come up with a number of test hypotheses.

Now you create a treatment, and test it against control. Oh no, it loses! Or oh no, there's no difference between the two variations! Now what?

You analyze the treatment, the results across segments, and improve your hypothesis. Then – you test again! Iterative testing is the name of the game. Be prepared to run many test rounds for each page. The odds of you solving all problems with the first test are slim! 10 tests to a sizable win is more like it.

Nobody knows which test is going to work. If we did, we wouldn't need testing! So inevitably some tests are either not going to produce a lift, or even perform worse than control. What matters is that you analyze each test result, update your test hypothesis and test again.

Remember - specific execution matters. Let's say you're trying to optimize for clarity. You re-write the body copy, headlines and CTAs. But – no lift. "Clarity is not an issue here", you might think. But there's also a good chance that the changes you implemented were still not clear enough. So you might want to try another test, using voice of the customer in the copy – the actual language they used in the surveys.

Tests lose all the time, and that's okay. It's about learning.

Some say only 1 out of 8 wins, some claim 75% of their tests win. Convert.com ran a query on their data and found that 70% of the A/B test performed by individuals without agencies don't lead to to any increase in conversion.
Ignore "market averages" for this kind of stuff as your average tester has

never done any conversion research, and is likely to have their testing methodology wrong as well. The same convert.com research also showed that using a marketing agency for A/B testing gives 235% more chance of a conversion increase. So competence clearly matter (of course, your average marketing agency is not very competent at CRO).

When you know that more than half of your tests are likely not to produce a lift, you will have new-found appreciation for learning. Always test a specific hypothesis! That way you never fully fail. With experience, you begin to realize that you sometimes learn even more from tests that did not perform as expected.

Matt Gershoff, Condutrics:

"Test is really data collection. Personally, I think the winner/loser vocabulary perhaps induces risk adversity."

Some people indeed fear that "losing" test would mean you did something wrong, and because of that your boss, client etc would not be happy with the performance. Doubt and uncertainty be start to cloud your thought process. The best way to overcome this is to be on the same page with everyone. Before you even get into testing, get everyone to together and agree that this is about learning.

The company profit is really just a by-product of successfully building on your customer theory.

Nazli Yuzak, Dell:

"There lies the reason why many tests fail: an incorrect initial hypothesis. From numerous tests, we've found that the hypothesis creation has a major impact on the way a test is run, what is tested, how long a test runs and just as important, who's being tested?"

What happens if test results are inconclusive?

Inconclusive tests are very common. It's when your treatment does not beat control, no statistical significance. This usually happens when your hypotheses is wrong, or your test wasn't bold or brave enough in shifting away from the original design, particularly on lower traffic sites.

So what do you do then? You analyze the segments.

Open up Google Analytics and see how the variations performed across different segments – new, returning, different browsers and devices, different traffic sources, other behavioral identifiers.

Quite often you will find that one of the variations was a confident winner in a specific segment. That's an insight you can build on! One or more segments may be over and under, or they may be cancelling out – the average is a lie. The segment level performance will help you (Note: in order to accurately assess performance across a segment, you again need a decent sample size!)

If you genuinely have a test which failed to move any segments, it's a crap test, assess how you came to this hypothesis and revise your whole hypothesis list.

And finally – get testing again!

What happens if test fails (Control wins)?

In short: Learn from the failure.

If you can't learn from the failure, you've designed a crap test. Next time you design, imagine all your stuff failing. What would you do?

If you don't know or you're not sure, get it changed so that a negative becomes useful. Failure itself at a creative or variable level should tell you something. On a failed test, always analyze the segmentation. One or more segments will be over and under – check for varied performance.

Now add the failure info to your customer theory. Look at it carefully – what does the failure tell you? Which element do you think drove the failure? If you know what failed (e.g. making the price bigger) then you have very useful information.

Perhaps you turned the handle the wrong way. Now look at all the data that you have, and brainstorm a new test.

Conclusion

Conversion optimization is not a set of tactics you can learn from a blog post. It's a process. Anyone who is not able to describe their CRO work as a systematic, repeatable process is a complete amateur.

www.ingramcontent.com/pod-product-compliance
Lightning Source LLC
Chambersburg PA
CBHW020516160726
47991CB00007B/2984